The Color of KENOSHA

2024 Edition

A Coloring Book for All-Ages from Kenosha, Wisconsin

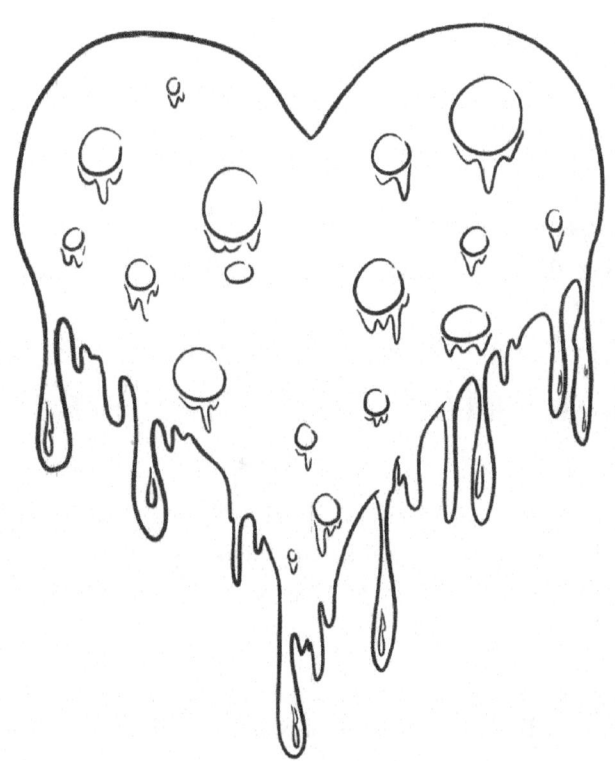

Created by
Donovan Scherer

The Color of Kenosha 2024:
A Coloring Book for All-Ages from Kenosha, Wisconsin

Text & Illustrations Copyright © 2024 by Donovan Scherer

Published in 2024 by Studio Moonfall LLC

All rights reserved.

This is a work of fiction. Names, characters, places, and incidents are products of the author's imagination or are used fictitiously. Any resemblance to actual events, locales, organizations, or persons, living or dead, is entirely coincidental.

No part of this book may be used or reproduced in any manner whatsoever without written permission, except in the case of brief quotations embodied in critical articles or reviews.

For information regarding permission, write to:

Studio Moonfall LLC
5031 7th Ave
Kenosha, WI 53140

ISBN: 978-1-942811-44-2

www.StudioMoonfall.com

Made in Kenosha

Welcome to the 2024 Color of Kenosha coloring book!

Holy moly! The newest Kenosha coloring book is here!

Studio Moonfall has been keeping busy with running events like the Kenosha Book Festival, selling books at the Kenosha Harbor Market, and putting together a brand new local coloring book for Pleasant Prairie.

While next year's schedule is looking a little simpler, we're going to be churning out all sorts of new books with rowdy raccoons, magical eggrolls, and of course, zombie beans. Stop by the shop and see what we're drawing up.

See you at Studio Moonfall!

Happy coloring,
Donovan

SPECIAL THANKS TO ALL THE BUSINESSES INVOLVED IN MAKING THIS BOOK

- Actor's Craft, LLC
- Alpaca Art
- Blue House Books
- Bradford Community Church
- Copy Center
- Cut Stone
- Daybreak Church
- Diver Dan's Scuba and Aquatic Center
- Dr. Destruction's Crimson Theatre
- Epique Realty
- EZ Pack n Ship
- Fear & Sunshine
- From Head To Tail
- Greetings from Pleasant Prairie
- Historic Military Impressions
- Hometown Meats
- Hope Council
- Kenosha Art Market
- Kenosha Book Festival
- Kenosha Harbor Market
- Kenosha Public Museum
- Kenosha Streetcar Society
- La Fogata & Waterfront Warehouse
- Little Europa
- Mars Cheese Castle
- Millhouse Auto Body
- Millie Bo Peep
- NAMI
- Red Rose's Bead Haven
- RK News Hallmark
- Roll With It
- Scrubby Duds Laundry Services
- Shalom Center
- Simply Spoken
- Studio Moonfall
- The Lettering Machine
- The Terrace
- Tree Frog Service LLC
- Visit Kenosha

LEARN MORE ABOUT ALL OF THEM AT: WWW.COLOROFKENOSHA.COM

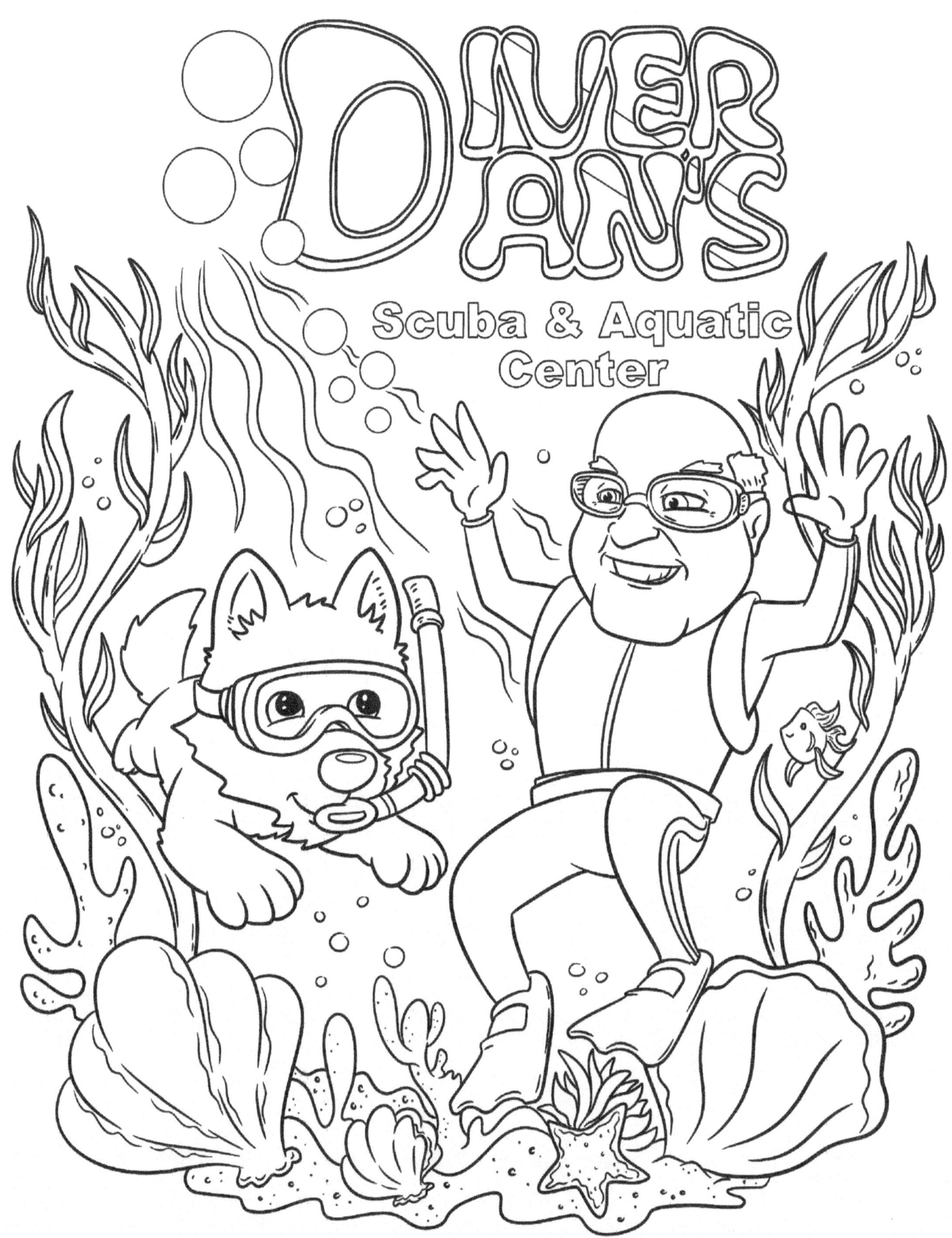

Kenosha Art Market

Original Art · Local Artists

Union Park, Kenosha

KENOSHA BOOK FESTIVAL

KENOSHA BOOK FESTIVAL 2024

- APR 28
- MAY 26
- JUNE 23
- JULY 28
- AUG 25
- SEP 22

• SHOP LOCAL •
• READ INDIE •

RK NEWS HALLMARK

SHALOM CENTER
BUILDING HOPE • IMPACTING LIVES

FOOD • SHELTER • GUIDANCE

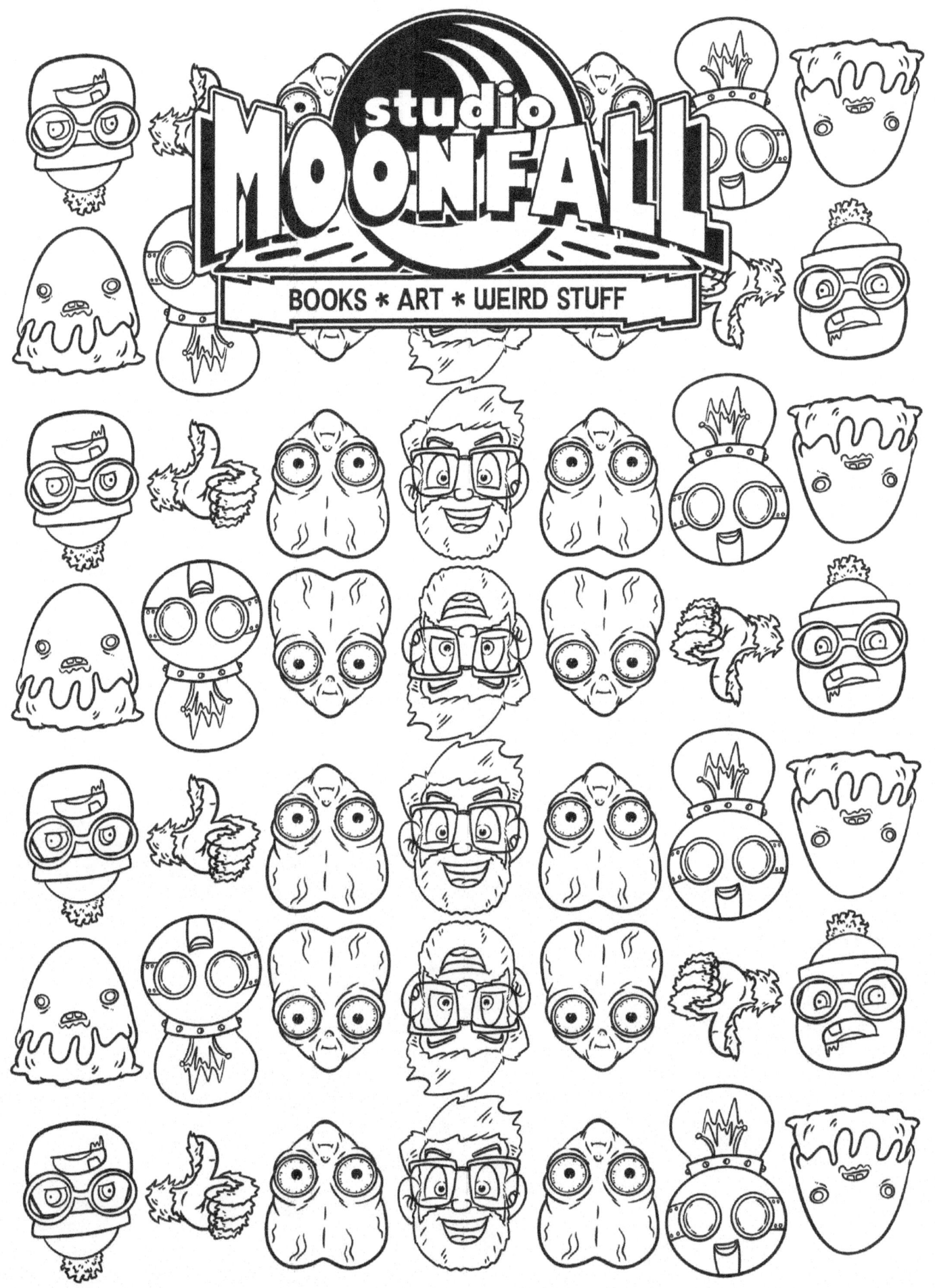

VISIT STUDIO MOONFALL AT 5031 7TH AVENUE IN KENOSHA!